LOVE WAS BORN AT CHRISTMAS

An Advent Booklet for Families

Susan Luttrell

LOVE WAS BORN AT CHRISTMAS

ISBN 0-89536-483-2   PRINTED IN U.S.A.

I dedicate this Advent booklet to my daughters, Elaine and Amy, who are as precious to me as they are to Jesus. It is my hope that parents will spend a few minutes each day with their children to share these Advent thoughts and Scriptures. May any blessings received from this booklet be reflected in the lives of our children and in the warmth of our homes. And may God be with you and yours during this Advent season.

Susan Luttrell

INTRODUCTION

Christmas is a wondrous time of year, and each year it seems as though the family is busier than ever. However, it is in the Christian family setting that the young child first discovers the true significance of the Christmas story. This Advent booklet has been prepared with these thoughts in mind.

The family will find a short meditation, with Scripture reference and a prayer, for each day of the Advent season. The subjects of the meditations and the vocabulary used have been selected carefully so that preschool children as well as adults may enjoy the Christmas story as it unfolds in word and picture.

It is suggested that the family use the devotions at the supper hour or at a special time each day. Only a few minutes are required for such sharing. After the daily meditation has been presented, the directions for the Advent manger scene are noted on the bottom of each page. This usually requires the coloring of one of the characters or animals in the scene, cutting around it, and pasting it onto the large paste page (matching the number of the cut-out to the number on the paste page).

When Christmas Eve arrives, the cut-out of the Christ child will be placed in the manger on the paste page. When this last cut-out is in place, the complete manger scene will have been a product of each child's own creativity and productivity. The excitement and anticipation of each day's addition will have helped to reinforce the true and blessed meaning of that first Christmas so long ago.

Susan Luttrell

Isaiah lived a long time before Jesus was born. But God told Isaiah that someday he would send his Son to live on the earth and be our Savior and friend. This made Isaiah happy, and he told everybody to get ready because Jesus was coming. We feel happy too when we think about Christmas and Jesus' coming. People joyfully celebrate Christmas because God gave the world his own Son, the very first Christmas gift. We make room for him in our hearts.

Isaiah 9:6

Prayer: O God, we know you did keep your promise to send your Son to save us. Help us to get ready in our hearts to celebrate his birthday. Amen.

Cut, color, and paste object number one.

Nazareth was a nice little city, but nothing very important ever happened there. Imagine how excited the people would have been if they had seen the angel God sent! But the angel didn't come to see all the people. He came to see just one young girl called Mary. He had a special message for her from God.

If you were just sitting in your house and suddenly an angel came to see you, all bright and shining, do you think you might be a little bit afraid? Well, Mary was. But the angel told her not to be afraid. "God is with you," he said. "God loves you very much." Then Mary wasn't afraid anymore.

Then the angel gave Mary the message from God. "You're going to have a little baby," he said. "You should call him Jesus. He will be such a special baby, Mary! He will be God's Son!" Wasn't that a wonderful message?

Luke 1:26-32, 38

Prayer: God, thank you for being faithful to Mary. Thank you for being faithful to us. Help us always to trust your promises. Give us the patience to wait for your blessings, and help us to celebrate while we wait. In Jesus' name. Amen.

Cut, color and paste object number two.

When a child is born into a family, one of the important things the parents do is choose a name for their child. How carefully they talk it over. Just any name will not do! They choose a name that they both love and one that is meaningful. Eagerly, the relatives and friends wait to hear what the baby's name will be. Just so, the name of Jesus holds special meaning to the Christian. How lovingly we speak the precious name of the Savior. With the song writer we joyfully sing,

Wonderful, wonderful,
Jesus is to me!
Counselor, Prince of peace,
Mighty God is He!
Saving me, keeping me
From all sin and shame,
Wonderful is my Redeemer,
Praise His name!

Luke 1:31, 32

Prayer: Dear God, thank you for our parents who so lovingly gave us our names, but thank you so much more for the name of Jesus and what that means to us. No name is more precious. In Jesus' name, Amen.

Cut, color and paste object number three.

Mary was so happy when the angel gave her God's message. She knew that God was using her to help keep the promise he had made to Isaiah a long time before. She hurried to visit her cousin Elizabeth and tell her the good news. And while Mary was at Elizabeth's house, she said a beautiful prayer to God. "Oh, how I praise the Lord. How I rejoice in God my Savior!"

Mary stayed with Elizabeth for a few months and then went back to her home. It was only a short time after this that Elizabeth gave birth to a baby boy who was later to be called John the Baptist.

Luke 1:46-55, 1:56-60

Prayer: Come, Lord Jesus, come. Bring us your love and peace and joy. Teach us how to celebrate and praise your name as Mary did. Amen.

Cut, color, and paste object number four.

We do not often speak of Joseph during the Advent weeks, but Joseph was an important part of the promise God made long ago. God promised Abraham that a very special blessing for the whole world would come from Abraham's nation. Through Joseph the promise was kept. Joseph's family can be traced all the way back to Abraham and, of course, Joseph was to be the father of Jesus — the very special blessing.

God could have kept his promise through some other relatives of Abraham. All we know is that he didn't. He chose Mary and Joseph on purpose. Mary and Joseph believed God's promises to them and remained faithful.

Luke 1:38

Prayer: Dear God, thank you for Mary and Joseph who obeyed you. Thank you for keeping your promise and sending us your Son. Amen.

Cut, color, and paste object number five.

After Mary and Joseph were married and waiting for Jesus to be born, the king decided to take a census (to count all his people) and said that everybody had to go to his home town to be counted. So Joseph and Mary had to go to Joseph's home town, Bethlehem. Mary was going to have her baby soon, and she rode to Bethlehem on a little donkey so she wouldn't get too tired. It was a long trip.

The hymn, "O Little Town of Bethlehem," is a favorite Christmas carol. The writer of the words is Phillips Brooks. He visited the fields of Bethlehem where it is believed the shepherds watched their flocks and heard the angel's message. As he thought about the gift of love God gave to all people that long ago night, he tried to imagine what it had been like. When Mr. Brooks returned to his home in Philadelphia, he often remembered the shepherd's fields near Bethlehem. Then one Christmas season he wrote the words of a song for the children of his church to sing at the Christmas program. He asked the church organist to compose the music.

The organist had trouble finding a tune he liked. Finally, before going to bed, he prayed about it. In the night he woke up, a tune in his mind. Quickly he wrote it down and the children sang the song.

Neither Mr. Brooks nor his organist ever expected anything great from the little song, but it has been a favorite carol for more than one hundred years.

Luke 2:1-5

Prayer: Dear Lord, thank you for Christmas songs that remind us of your great love for us. Thank you for taking our little gifts and making them so much more. Amen.

Cut, color, and paste object number six.

When Joseph and Mary finally got to Bethlehem, they couldn't find any place to stay. Finally Joseph said to an innkeeper, "Please help us. My wife is going to have a baby very soon." "Well," said the innkeeper, "I guess you can stay in my stable with the animals." So, there in the stable with the cows and the sheep and the little donkey, God kept his promise. Jesus, God's Son, was born.

Look at this manger. Look closely. Do you see clean, soft sheets and a firm mattress? Do you see baby lotion, powder, or a clean hospital room? No, not for this special baby, Jesus. Jesus sleeps in a manger. A manger is a feeding trough for animals. How wonderful to see. A baby who came to earth to bring love and the bread of life (salvation) sleeps in a feeding trough! How excitingly God reveals his purpose for this sweet child.

Luke 2:6

Prayer: Be near me, Lord Jesus,
       I ask Thee to stay
  Close by me forever
       And love me, I pray;
  Bless all the dear children
       In Thy tender care,
  And take us to heaven
       To live with Thee there. Amen.

Cut, color, and paste object number seven.

Franz Gruber was an organist in his church in Oberndorf, Austria, in 1818. One day, as he started to practice for a Christmas Eve service, he was very sad and upset because the old organ would not make a sound.

Josef Mohr, the minister of the church, saw Franz's disappointment and agreed with Franz that there was not enough time to have it repaired. However, he handed Franz a slip of paper with words for a song on it and asked Franz if he would write the music to it. Franz could then play the song on his guitar while the people sang it on Christmas Eve.

When the church bells tolled that Christmas Eve, there was no sound of organ music to greet them. However, their worship was wonderfully rich with the sound of a guitar and the words of "Silent Night, Holy Night." Even today we cherish this carol as a remembrance of God's love as it came to us that silent night so long ago.

John 3:16

Prayer: O God, we thank you again for songs that have blessed your people through the years. We wait with hope and love again for the celebration of that silent night of long ago. Amen.

Cut, color, and paste object number eight.

Isn't Christmas exciting! Decorations, parties, and gifts are everywhere. In the midst of these wonderful things, let's stop and think of the very first Christmas gift. It was given a long time ago and in a far away land. That first gift wasn't wrapped in gay ribbon and paper. It didn't take hours of shopping, wrapping, or wondering. It was such a simple gift — a small baby wrapped in plain cloth and lying in a manger. Yet this gift was the greatest ever given and was given to all people. (No matter what size they are, color or age.) This baby Jesus was the perfect gift of love given to us by God.

This gift is the real reason we give each other Christmas presents. They remind us of the great gift God gave us when he sent Jesus to live and die and rise again for us.

Meditation: "The First Gift of Christmas"
The first Christmas Gift ever given
Wasn't bought in a mart or a shop,
And it wasn't encased in gay wrapping
With a bright ribbon bow on the top.
The first gift of Christmas was given
In a manger lowly and bare,
And a blanket was the lone wrapping
of this gift so priceless and fair.
God gave the first Gift of Christmas,
A most Holy and Wonderful One,
When He looked down in mercy and goodness
And gave us the Gift of His Son!
John Gilbert

Prayer: Dear God, thank you for the wonderful gift of Jesus and the love you sent to us through him. May the gifts we give to others this year be gifts of love and kindness. Amen.

Cut, color, and paste object number nine.

To a small number of shepherds who were taking care of their sheep on the hillsides of Bethlehem, angels came to announce that God had kept his promise to his people. The sky was flooded with light shining down on the shepherds below. Imagine how frightened and worried the shepherds were! "Don't be afraid!" the angel said. "I bring you the most joyful news ever announced, and it is for everyone! The Savior — yes, the Messiah, the Lord — has been born tonight in Bethlehem! How will you recognize him? You will find a baby wrapped in a blanket lying in a manger!"

Then the angel was joined by hundreds of angels and they sang out: "Glory to God in the highest heaven — and peace on earth for all those pleasing him."

After hearing this, the shepherds ran to the village to see this for themselves. Their hearts were pounding loudly as they found the stable and peered inside. Never had they seen such a sight. Inside as they knelt before the baby, they knew that what the angel had told them was true. Here was the Savior, Christ the Lord.

Luke 2:8-16

Prayer: Dear Lord, thanks be to you for giving the good news of Christ's birth to the shepherds long ago and to all of us today. Amen.

Cut, color, and paste object number ten.

Has your mother or father ever said to you, "Be an angel"? If they have, you know they meant for you to keep quiet, or sit still, or do a favor. Think about the angels in the Christmas story. They weren't quiet; they were big, bright and frightening. They arrived in a blaze of light that filled the sky with God's glory. Their mission was a super special one — to tell of the birth of Jesus. They were important messengers from God who brought the good news of peace and shouted his praises.

We have the same job to do. So, be an angel and spread the Good News of our Savior. You won't be able to light up the sky, but you might give a little light to someone's life. So, be an Angel!

Luke 2:9-14

Prayer: God, thank you for sending the angels to announce the birth of Jesus. Thank you for giving us your Word to share with others. Help us to be your "angels" too. Amen.

Cut, color, and paste object number eleven.

The shepherds, after visiting the stable, could have kept secret what they saw and could have gone straight back to their flocks without telling anyone. After all, the angel did come to just them. But thankfully they did not keep what they had seen a secret. They chose to tell everybody they saw. "Listen, everybody!" they said. "God is good. He has sent his Son. Jesus is born!" Don't you like to tell people that good news too? Christmas can be every day of the year if we do as the shepherds did and share the good news of Jesus Christ with everybody we meet.

Luke 2:17-20

Prayer: God, help us to share the good news with our friends and family. Help us to share the best news the world could ever want! Amen.

Cut, color, and paste object number twelve.

On the night Jesus was born, a very special light appeared in the sky. It was a star — far, far away, and greatly mysterious. In giving his promise about the coming of Jesus, God mentioned a star. One of God's prophets told the people that a star from Jacob would one day come to be the ruler of Israel (Numbers 24:17).

The star the prophet talked about was Jesus. When he came to earth, he was no longer far away or mysterious like the star that shone on Christmas Eve. He had come to live with and teach the people about love and eternal life.

We no longer need to wonder about Jacob's star that the people told about. We know that this star is Jesus Christ, God's only begotten Son.

Matthew 2:1, 2

Prayer: O God, when we think of that mysterious star that shone over Bethlehem, help us to think of the star that the prophet talked about. Help us to see Jesus as the light of the world and help us to share this light with others. Amen.

Cut, color, and paste object number thirteen.

Just a few people saw Baby Jesus on that first Christmas day: Mary and Joseph, the shepherds, and maybe some of the people the shepherds told. But there were some other people wanting to see him, and they were on their way. God sent a star to guide the Wise Men to Jesus.

They had to travel a long way. The Bible doesn't tell us which country the Wise Men came from, only that it was in the East. Legends and stories about these men often say that each Wise Man was from a different land. In famous paintings, artists have painted the Wise Men as three kings dressed in rich robes, wearing crowns, and carrying costly gifts. One king is an Ethopian, a black man; one is olive skinned, an Oriental; and one is white skinned. In this way, these artists tried to show that Jesus was given to all people for all times. God certainly intended just that!

Matthew 2:1-10

Prayer: Dear Father, when the Wise Men saw the light of Jesus' star, they knew that a great king had been born. Thank you for sending Jesus to save all people everywhere. Amen.

Cut, color, and paste object number fourteen.

When at last the Wise Men finally found Baby Jesus, they knelt down and worshiped him. Those three big men knelt down to worship a small baby. But they knew just how special that small baby was! The Wise Men were very rich, and they brought Jesus beautiful gifts. One of the gifts was gold. Another was incense that smelled good when it was lighted. The third was a costly perfume. They were able to bring rich gifts, but we can give gifts to Jesus too. By giving gifts of love to poor and sad people, we are giving gifts to him.

Matthew 2:11

Prayer: Father, help us always to give gifts of love to those we meet and to honor Jesus as our Savior. We know we can never give a gift as wonderful as your gift of Baby Jesus. Amen.

Cut, color, and paste object number fifteen.

"Joy to the World" is a Christmas carol that surely describes the joy we find in the manger scene. This lovely song was first heard as a poem and later set to music. A minister, Isaac Watts, devoted his life to the writing of hymns after a serious illness forced him to retire.

One of his most stirring and inspiring poems was set to music and at Christmas the wonderful carol, "Joy to The World," is heard throughout the land.

Joy to the world!
The Lord is come;
Let earth receive her King;
Let every heart prepare him room,
And heaven and nature sing,
And heaven and nature sing,
And heaven, and heaven and nature sing.

He rules the world
With truth and grace,
And makes the nations prove
The glories of his righteousness,
And wonders of his love
And wonders of his love
And wonders, wonders, of his love.

Prayer: Our Father, thank you for the joy of Christmas, and the carols we sing. We pray our joy will be shared with others now and always. Amen.

Cut, color, and paste object number sixteen.

Aren't birthday parties exciting! Sometimes it seems so hard to wait from one year to the next. Christmas is a very special birthday celebration. We celebrate not only the birth of baby Jesus, but Jesus our Savior. He's the only Savior we have and he's here in our hearts and the lives of all those who love him. So we can have a birthday party for Jesus by having a party with each other.

As we wait for Christmas let's remember what we're waiting for. We're waiting to give a party for Jesus, not get a party for ourselves. We're waiting to celebrate once more God's very special gift to us — his Son, our Savior.

What can I give Him, poor as I am?
If I were a shepherd,
I would bring a lamb;
If I were a wise man,
I would do my part,
Yet what can I give Him;
Give my heart.

Christina G. Rosetti

Prayer: Dear God, joy fills us at Christmas time and sometimes it seems we can hardly wait. Give us patience and help us remember that this is a celebration of love. Amen.

Cut, color, and paste object number seventeen.

Another object of great joy at Christmas is the Christmas tree. Christmas trees are usually evergreens decked out with gay colored balls, tinsel, and bright lights. It is no accident that the evergreen was chosen to be the Christmas tree. Because the evergreen is green all year long, it represents the fact that Jesus is forever and will never die.

The star has traditionally been used on top the tree. This is probably due to the fact that on that first Christmas Eve so long ago the shepherds saw the Bethlehem star shining through the trees of Judea. What a wonderful reminder of that glorious star!

We also know that Jesus died on a cross made from a tree. Our tree reminds us that he died so our sins might be forgiven.

The Christmas Tree

O lovely way to celebrate your birth
Whose Birth Star glistened through Judea's
trees;
Whom Joseph taught the skillful use of these;
Who, on a tree, once overcame the earth!
Grant then your blessing, Friend of trees,
we pray
On those who deck green boughs for Christmas
Day!

Violet Alleyn Storey

Prayer: Come, O Jesus, into our hearts and let your light shine in our lives just as the lights glow on our Christmas tree. Amen.

Cut, color, and paste object number eighteen.

St. Paul wrote many letters to people in the early churches. He wanted the congregations to know he was thinking about them and praying for them. He wanted to constantly remind them of God's love and care for them. When we receive cards and letters during the Christmas season, we are happy to know our friends have remembered us. If we're unhappy or worried, a note or card can give us strength.

God wants us to love everyone, but it's very important that we care about our fellow Christians — not only fellow Christians in our community church, but Christians everywhere. Perhaps this Christmas we might make a special effort to send a word of love or cheer to a fellow Christian who needs our concern and encouragement. Can you think of someone?

1 Thessalonians 5:11

Prayer: Dear God, thank you for all the people who love us and encourage us. Help us show love and concern for others. Amen.

Cut, color, and paste object number nineteen.

Each year during the Christmas season, we Christians have a chance to share the joy we have. Read this story to see how one Christian boy was able to share his joy.

Mark dropped his books on the kitchen table and slid into the chair. "You're late from school," his mother said. "You want some milk and cookies?" "I'm not hungry," Mark said. "Are you sick?" his mother asked. "Nope." Mark took a big breath. "Tom's the new boy in school. His father left home last week, and his mother says there won't be enough money for Christmas gifts. Mark doesn't really care, but he has a little sister and brother. He thinks they'll be disappointed without Christmas presents."

Would you like to know what Mark did? He took some of the money he had been saving and bought little gifts for Tom's sister and brother. Mark's mother baked Christmas cookies and some special bread. Mark took them to Tom's house.

Is there a special way you can show someone kindness this Christmas season?

Hebrews 10:24

Prayer: Dear Father, thank you for the good things you give us. Help us to be willing to show our love to those who need help. Amen.

Cut, color, and paste object number twenty.

Christmas Is Love . . .

What greater love could exist than the love of God for man; the love which prompted God to send his Son to Earth, to be born in humbleness and obscurity, in order that men might be saved? "And she brought forth her firstborn Son, and wrapped him in swaddling clothes, and laid him in a manger . . ." Can we ever thank God enough for his infinite love of us? For coming down to us? Do we realize fully that he is truly "the God of Love"?

As long as we try to keep in our hearts a spark of that Divine Love; love for God and for our neighbor . . . Christmas is love.

James Kellar

John 3:16

Prayer: Thank you, Father, for the gift of love in Jesus Christ that you have given to us. We can receive no greater gift. Amen.

Cut, color, and paste object number twenty-one.

Christmas Is Hope . . .

How long the world had waited for the coming of the Messiah! How often they had hoped for the day!

And then one long-ago night in Bethlehem, their hearts were gladdened by a brilliant star in the East . . . a heavenly sign that the birth of the Christ Child was near.

"And the angel said to them, 'Fear not, for behold, I bring you glad tidings of great joy . . .' "

The star of Bethlehem still should shine as radiantly and brightly as ever in our hearts and souls as we anticipate his coming once again!

For as long as we renew our faith, and hope, and welcome the Christ Child with the same triumphant joy which the shepherds felt on that first Christmas night . . . Christmas is hope.

James Kellar

Romans 15:13

Prayer: O Lord, fill us with hope as we wait for Christmas Day. Make this a Christmas of hope for everyone. Amen.

Cut, color, and paste object number twenty-two.

Christmas Is Peace . . .

"Peace on earth to men of good will . . ." Picture the quiet hills of Bethlehem, the radiant star, the peaceful stable with the Infant King; Mary, his mother; and Joseph. Tranquility, peace, calm, serenity.

What a difference from our wild activity, the noise, confusion, and disorder of our modern world!

It can be most helpful to withdraw for a moment or two from all this hustle and bustle into some quiet church or chapel to think about the birth of the Christ Child, the miracle of his coming, the love he has for all people!

How rewarding, how satisfying to feel the presence of God in our hearts and souls! If we recapture the quiet and peacefulness of that first Christmas when the Prince of Peace was born to us . . . Christmas is Peace.

James Kellar

John 20:21

Prayer: Let there be peace on earth, my Father, and let that peace begin with me. Amen.

Cut, color, and paste object number twenty-three.

At last! At last! The time is here and we are ready. **Ready for what?** Ready for the Christ Child to be born again in our hearts. Ready to say thank you for a promise made long ago and never broken. Ready to sing and praise God's name for the joy and hope that each Christmas Eve brings. Ready to become quiet and peaceful so that we can once again listen to the wonderful story of Jesus' birth and know it is a story given to each of us.

Love came down at Christmas,
Love all lovely, Love Divine;
Love was born at Christmas,
Star and Angels gave the sign.

Christina Rossetti

Prayer: Come, Baby Jesus. Come into our hearts this day. Show us your love and how we can give it to others. Bless our home and family and those far away. Amen.

Cut, color, and paste object number twenty-four.

www.ingramcontent.com/pod-product-compliance
Lightning Source LLC
Chambersburg PA
CBHW071806020426
42331CB00008B/2416